Wolfert Webber

Golden Dreams

Washington Irving

16pt

Read How You Want

LARGE PRINT BOOKS, BRAILLE & DAISY

In the year of grace one thousand seven hundred and – blank – for I do not remember the precise date; however, it was somewhere in the early part of the last century, – there lived in the ancient city of the Manhattoes a worthy burgher, Wolfert Webber by name. He was descended from old Cobus Webber of the Brill[1] in Holland, one of the original settlers, famous for introducing the cultivation of cabbages, and who came over to the province during the protectorship of Oloffe Van Kortlandt, otherwise called "the Dreamer."

The field in which Cobus Webber first planted himself and his cabbages had remained ever since in the family, who continued in the same line of husbandry with that praiseworthy perseverance for which our Dutch burghers are noted. The whole family genius, during several generations, was devoted to the study and development of this one noble vegetable, and to this concentration of intellect may doubtless

---

[1] The Brill is a fortified seaport of Holland, on the Meuse River, near Rotterdam.

be ascribed the prodigious renown to which the Webber cabbages attained.

The Webber dynasty continued in uninterrupted succession, and never did a line give more unquestionable proofs of legitimacy. The eldest son succeeded to the looks as well as the territory of his sire, and had the portraits of this line of tranquil potentates been taken, they would have presented a row of heads marvelously resembling, in shape and magnitude, the vegetables over which they reigned.

The seat of government continued unchanged in the family mansion, – a Dutch-built house, with a front, or rather gable end, of yellow brick, tapering to a point, with the customary iron weathercock at the top. Everything about the building bore the air of long-settled ease and security. Flights of martins peopled the little coops nailed against its walls, and swallows built their nests under the eaves, and everyone knows that these house-loving birds bring good luck to the dwelling where they take up their abode. In a bright summer morning in early summer, it was delectable to hear their cheerful notes as they sported about in the pure, sweet air, chirping forth, as it were, the greatness and prosperity of the Webbers.

Thus quietly and comfortably did this excellent family vegetate under the shade of a mighty buttonwood tree, which by little and little grew so great as entirely to overshadow their palace. The city gradually spread its suburbs round their domain. Houses sprang up to interrupt their prospects. The rural lanes in the vicinity began to grow into the bustle and populousness of streets; in short, with all the habits of rustic life they began to find themselves the inhabitants of a city. Still, however, they maintained their hereditary character and hereditary possessions, with all the tenacity of petty German princes in the midst of the empire. Wolfert was the last of the line, and succeeded to the patriarchal bench at the door, under the family tree, and swayed the scepter of his fathers, – a kind of rural potentate in the midst of the metropolis.

To share the cares and sweets of sovereignty he had taken unto himself a helpmate, one of that excellent kind called "stirring women"; that is to say, she was one of those notable little housewives who are always busy where there is nothing to do. Her activity, however, took one particular direction, – her whole life seemed devoted to intense knitting; whether at home or abroad, walking or sitting, her needles were continually in motion, and it is even affirmed that by her unwearied industry she very nearly supplied her household with stockings throughout the year. This worthy couple were blessed with one daughter who was brought up with great tenderness and care; uncommon pains had been taken with her education, so that she could stitch in every variety of way, make all kinds of pickles and preserves, and mark her own name on a sampler. The influence of her taste was seen also in the family garden, where the ornamental began to mingle with the useful; whole rows of fiery marigolds and splendid hollyhocks bordered the cabbage beds, and gigantic sunflowers lolled their broad, jolly faces over the fences, seeming to ogle most affectionately the passersby.

Thus reigned and vegetated Wolfert Webber over his paternal acres, peacefully and contentedly. Not but that, like all other sovereigns, he had his occasional cares and vexations. The growth of his native city sometimes caused him annoyance. His little territory gradually became hemmed in by streets and houses, which intercepted air and sunshine. He was now and then subjected to the eruptions of the border population that infest the streets of a metropolis, who would make midnight forays into his dominions, and carry off captive whole platoons of his noblest subjects. Vagrant swine would make a descent, too, now and then, when the gate was left open, and lay all waste before them; and mischievous urchins would decapitate the illustrious sunflowers, the glory of the garden, as they lolled their heads so fondly over the walls. Still all these were petty grievances, which might now and then ruffle the surface of his mind, as a summer breeze will ruffle the surface of a mill pond, but they could not disturb the deep-seated quiet of his soul. He would but seize a trusty staff that stood behind the door, issue suddenly out, and anoint the back of the aggressor, whether pig or urchin, and then return within doors, marvelously refreshed and tranquilized.

The chief cause of anxiety to honest Wolfert, however, was the growing prosperity of the city. The expenses of living doubled and trebled, but he could not double and treble the magnitude of his cabbages, and the number of competitors prevented the increase of price; thus, therefore, while everyone around him grew richer, Wolfert grew poorer, and he could not, for the life of him, perceive how the evil was to be remedied.

This growing care, which increased from day to day, had its gradual effect upon our worthy burgher, insomuch that it at length implanted two or three wrinkles in his brow, things unknown before in the family of the Webbers, and it seemed to pinch up the corners of his cocked hat into an expression of anxiety totally opposite to the tranquil, broad-brimmed, low-crowned beavers of his illustrious progenitors.

Perhaps even this would not have materially disturbed the serenity of his mind had he had only himself and his wife to care for; but there was his daughter gradually growing to maturity, and all the world knows that when daughters begin to ripen, no fruit nor flower requires so much looking after. I have no talent at describing female charms, else fain would I depict the progress of this little Dutch beauty: how her blue eyes grew deeper and deeper, and her cherry lips redder and redder, and how she ripened and ripened, and rounded and rounded, in the opening breath of sixteen summers, until, in her seventeenth spring, she seemed ready to burst out of her bodice, like a half-blown rosebud.

Ah, well-a-day! Could I but show her as she was then, tricked out on a Sunday morning in the hereditary finery of the old Dutch clothespress, of which her mother had confided to her the key! The wedding dress of her grandmother, modernized for use, with sundry ornaments, handed down as heirlooms in the family. Her pale brown hair smoothed with buttermilk in flat, waving lines on each side of her fair forehead. The chain of yellow, virgin gold that encircled her neck; the little cross that just rested at the entrance of a soft valley of happiness, as if it would sanctify the place. The – but pooh! it is not for an old man like me to be prosing about female beauty; suffice it to say, Amy had attained her seventeenth year. Long since had her sampler exhibited hearts in couples desperately transfixed with arrows, and true lovers' knots worked in deep blue silk, and it was evident she began to languish for some more interesting occupation than the rearing of sunflowers or pickling of cucumbers.

At this critical period of female existence, when the heart within a damsel's bosom, like its emblem, the miniature which hangs without, is apt to be engrossed by a single image, a new visitor began to make his appearance under the roof of Wolfert Webber. This was Dirk Waldron, the only son of a poor widow, but who could boast of more fathers than any lad in the province, for his mother had had four husbands, and this only child, so that, though born in her last wedlock, he might fairly claim to be the tardy fruit of a long course of cultivation. This son of four fathers united the merits and the vigor of all his sires. If he had not had a great family before him he seemed likely to have a great one after him, for you had only to look at the fresh, buxom youth to see that he was formed to be the founder of a mighty race.

This youngster gradually became an intimate visitor of the family. He talked little, but he sat long. He filled the father's pipe when it was empty, gathered up the mother's knitting needle, or ball of worsted, when it fell to the ground, stroked the sleek coat of the tortoiseshell cat, and replenished the teapot for the daughter from the bright copper kettle that sang before the fire. All these quiet little offices may seem of trifling import, but when true love is translated into Low Dutch it is in this way that it eloquently expresses itself. They were not lost upon the Webber family. The winning youngster found marvelous favor in the eyes of the mother; the tortoiseshell cat, albeit the most staid and demure of her kind, gave indubitable signs of approbation of his visits; the teakettle seemed to sing out a cheering note of welcome at his approach; and if the sly glances of the daughter might be rightly read, as she sat bridling and dimpling, and sewing by her mother's side, she was not a whit behind Dame Webber, or grimalkin, or the teakettle, in good will.

Wolfert alone saw nothing of what was going on. Profoundly wrapt up in meditation on the growth of the city and his cabbages, he sat looking in the fire, and puffing his pipe in silence. One night, however, as the gentle Amy, according to custom, lighted her lover to the outer door, and he, according to custom, took his parting salute, the smack resounded so vigorously through the long, silent entry as to startle even the dull ear of Wolfert. He was slowly roused to a new source of anxiety. It had never entered into his head that this mere child, who, as it seemed, but the other day had been climbing about his knees and playing with dolls and baby houses, could all at once be thinking of lovers and matrimony. He rubbed his eyes, examined into the fact, and really found that while he had been dreaming of other matters, she had actually grown to be a woman, and, what was worse, had fallen in love. Here arose new cares for Wolfert. He was a kind father, but he was a prudent man. The young man was a lively, stirring lad, but then he had neither money nor land. Wolfert's ideas all ran in one channel, and he saw no alternative in case of a marriage but to portion off the young couple with a corner of his cabbage garden, the whole of which was barely sufficient for the support of his family.

Like a prudent father, therefore, he determined to nip this passion in the bud, and forbade the youngster the house, though sorely did it go against his fatherly heart, and many a silent tear did it cause in the bright eye of his daughter. She showed herself, however, a pattern of filial piety and obedience. She never pouted and sulked; she never flew in the face of parental authority; she never flew into a passion, nor fell into hysterics, as many romantic, novel-read young ladies would do. Not she, indeed. She was none such heroical, rebellious trumpery, I'll warrant ye. On the contrary, she acquiesced like an obedient daughter, shut the street door in her lover's face, and if ever she did grant him an interview, it was either out of the kitchen window or over the garden fence.

Wolfert was deeply cogitating these matters in his mind, and his brow wrinkled with unusual care, as he wended his way one Saturday afternoon to a rural inn, about two miles from the city. It was a favorite resort of the Dutch part of the community, from being always held by a Dutch line of landlords, and retaining an air and relish of the good old times. It was a Dutch-built house, that had probably been a country seat of some opulent burgher in the early time of the settlement. It stood near a point of land called Corlear's Hook,[2] which stretches out into the Sound, and against which the tide, at its flux and reflux, sets with

---

2 A point of land at the bend of the East River below Grand Street, New York City.

extraordinary rapidity. The venerable and somewhat crazy mansion was distinguished from afar by a grove of elms and sycamores that seemed to wave a hospitable invitation, while a few weeping willows, with their dank, drooping foliage, resembling falling waters, gave an idea of coolness that rendered it an attractive spot during the heats of summer.

Here, therefore, as I said, resorted many of the old inhabitants of the Manhattoes, where, while some played at shuffle board[3] and quoits,[4] and ninepins, others smoked a deliberate pipe, and talked over public affairs.

It was on a blustering autumnal afternoon that Wolfert made his visit to the inn. The grove of elms and willows was stripped of its leaves, which whirled in rustling eddies about the fields. The

---

3 A game played by pushing or shaking pieces of money or metal so as to make them reach certain marks on a board.

4 A game played by pitching a flattened, ring-shaped piece of iron, called a quoit, at a fixed object.

ninepin alley was deserted, for the premature chilliness of the day had driven the company within doors. As it was Saturday afternoon the habitual club was in session, composed principally of regular Dutch burghers, though mingled occasionally with persons of various character and country, as is natural in a place of such motley population.

Beside the fireplace, in a huge, leather-bottomed armchair, sat the dictator of this little world, the venerable Rem, or, as it was pronounced, Ramm" Rapelye. He was a man of Walloon[5] race, and illustrious for the antiquity of his line, his great-grandmother having been the first white child born in the province. But he was still more illustrious for his wealth and dignity. He had long filled the noble office of alderman, and was a man to whom the governor himself took off his hat. He had maintained possession of

---

[5] A people of French origin, inhabiting the frontiers between France and Flanders. A colony of one hundred and ten Walloons came to New York in 1624.

the leather-bottomed chair from time immemorial, and had gradually waxed in bulk as he sat in his seat of government, until in the course of years he filled its whole magnitude. His word was decisive with his subjects, for he was so rich a man that he was never expected to support any opinion by argument. The landlord waited on him with peculiar officiousness, – not that he paid better than his neighbors, but then the coin of a rich man seems always to be so much more acceptable. The landlord had ever a pleasant word and a joke to insinuate in the ear of the august Ramm. It is true Ramm never laughed, and, indeed, ever maintained a mastiff-like gravity and even surliness of aspect; yet he now and then rewarded mine host with a token of approbation, which, though nothing more nor less than a kind of grunt, still delighted the landlord more than a broad laugh from a poorer man.

"This will be a rough night for the money diggers," said mine host, as a gust of wind bowled round the house and rattled at the windows.

"What! are they at their works again?" said an English half-pay captain, with one eye, who was a very frequent attendant at the inn.

"Aye are they," said the landlord, "and well may they be. They've had luck of late. They say a great pot of money has been dug up in the fields just behind Stuyvesant's orchard. Folks think it must have been buried there in old times by Peter Stuyvesant, the Dutch governor."

"Fudge!" said the one-eyed man of war, as he added a small portion of water to a bottom of brandy.

"Well, you may believe it or not, as you please," said mine host, somewhat nettled, "but everybody knows that the old governor buried a great deal of his money at the time of the Dutch troubles, when the English redcoats seized on the province. They say, too, the old gentleman walks, aye, and in the very same dress that he wears in the picture that hangs up in the family house."

"Fudge!" said the half-pay officer.

"Fudge, if you please! But didn't Corney Van Zandt see him at midnight, stalking about in the meadow with his wooden leg, and a drawn sword in his hand, that flashed like fire? And what can he be walking for but because people have been troubling the place where he buried his money in old times?"

Here the landlord was interrupted by several guttural sounds from Ramm Rapelye, betokening that he was laboring with the unusual production of an idea. As he was too great a man to be slighted by a prudent publican, mine host respectfully paused until he should deliver himself. The corpulent frame of this mighty burgher now gave all the symptoms of a volcanic mountain on the point of an eruption. First there was a certain heaving of the abdomen, not unlike an earthquake; then was emitted a cloud of tobacco smoke from that crater, his mouth; then there was a kind of rattle in the throat, as if the idea were working its way up through a region of phlegm; then there were several disjointed members of a sentence thrown out, ending in a cough; at length his voice forced its way into a slow, but absolute tone of a man who feels the weight of his purse, if not of his ideas, every portion of his speech being marked by a testy puff of tobacco smoke.

"Who talks of old Peter Stuyvesant's walking? (puff). Have people no respect for persons? (puff – puff). Peter Stuyvesant knew better what to do with his money than to bury it (puff). I know the Stuyvesant family (puff), every one of them (puff); not a more respectable family in the province (puff) – old standards (puff) – warm householders (puff) – none of your upstarts (puff – puff – puff). Don't talk to me of Peter Stuyvesant's walking (puff – puff – puff – puff)."

Here the redoubtable Ramm contracted his brow, clasped up his mouth till it wrinkled at each corner, and redoubled his smoking with such vehemence that the cloudy volumes soon wreathed round his head, as the smoke envelops the awful summit of Mount Aetna.

A general silence followed the sudden rebuke of this very rich man. The subject, however, was too interesting to be readily abandoned. The conversation soon broke forth again from the lips of Peechy Prauw Van Hook, the chronicler of the club, one of those prosing, narrative old men who seem to be troubled with an incontinence of words as they grow old.

Peechy could, at any time, tell as many stories in an evening as his hearers could digest in a month. He now resumed the conversation by affirming that, to his knowledge, money had, at different times, been digged up in various parts of the island. The lucky persons who had discovered them had always dreamed of them three times beforehand, and, what was worthy of remark, those treasures had never been found but by some descendant of the good old Dutch families, which clearly proved that they had been buried by Dutchmen in the olden time.

"Fiddlestick with your Dutchmen!" cried the half-pay officer. "The Dutch had nothing to do with them. They were all buried by Kidd the pirate, and his crew."

Here a keynote was touched that roused the whole company. The name of Captain Kidd was like a talisman in those times, and was associated with a thousand marvelous stories.

The half-pay officer took the lead, and in his narrations fathered upon Kidd all the plunderings and exploits of Morgan,[6] Black beard,[7] and the whole list of bloody buccaneers.

The officer was a man of great weight among the peaceable members of the club, by reason of his warlike character and gunpowder tales. All his golden stories of Kidd, however, and of the booty he had buried, were obstinately rivaled by the tales of Peechy Prauw, who, rather than suffer

---

[6] Sir Henry Morgan (1637-90), a noted Welsh buccaneer. He was captured and sent to England for trial, but Charles II., instead of punishing him, knighted him, and subsequently appointed him governor of Jamaica.

[7] Edward Teach, one of the most cruel of the pirates, took command of a pirate ship in 1717, and thereafter committed all sorts of atrocities until he was slain by Lieutenant Maynard in 1718. His nickname of "Blackbeard" was given him because of his black beard.

his Dutch progenitors to be eclipsed by a foreign freebooter, enriched every field and shore in the neighborhood with the hidden wealth of Peter Stuyvesant and his contemporaries.

Not a word of this conversation was lost upon Wolfert Webber. He returned pensively home, full of magnificent ideas. The soil of his native island seemed to be turned into gold dust, and every field to teem with treasure. His head almost reeled at the thought how often he must have heedlessly rambled over places where countless sums lay, scarcely covered by the turf beneath his feet. His mind was in an uproar with this whirl of new ideas. As he came in sight of the venerable mansion of his forefathers, and the little realm where the Webbers had so long and so contentedly flourished, his gorge rose at the narrowness of his destiny.

"Unlucky Wolfert!" exclaimed he; "others can go to bed and dream themselves into whole mines of wealth; they have but to seize a spade in the morning, and turn up doubloons[8] like potatoes; but thou must dream of hardships, and rise to poverty, must dig thy field from year's end to year's end, and yet raise nothing but cabbages!"

Wolfert Webber went to bed with a heavy heart, and it was long before the golden visions that disturbed his brain permitted him to sink into repose. The same visions, however, extended into his sleeping thoughts, and assumed a more definite form. He dreamed that he had discovered an immense treasure in the center of his garden. At every stroke of the spade he laid bare a golden ingot; diamond crosses sparkled out of the dust; bags of money turned up their bellies, corpulent with pieces-of-eight[9] or venerable doubloons; and chests wedged close with

---

[8] Spanish gold coins, equivalent to $15.60.

[9] Spanish coins, worth about $1 each.

moidores,[10] ducats,[11] and pistareens,[12] yawned before his ravished eyes, and vomited forth their glittering contents.

Wolfert awoke a poorer man than ever. He had no heart to go about his daily concerns, which appeared so paltry and profitless, but sat all day long in the chimney corner, picturing to himself ingots and heaps of gold in the fire. The next night his dream was repeated. He was again in his garden digging, and laying open stores of hidden wealth. There was something very singular in this repetition. He passed another day of reverie, and though it was cleaning day, and the house, as usual in Dutch households, completely topsy-turvy, yet he sat unmoved amidst the general uproar.

The third night he went to bed with a palpitating heart. He put on his red nightcap wrong side outward, for good

---

10 Portuguese gold coins, valued at $6.50.

11 Coins of gold and silver, valued at $2 and $1 respectively.

12 Spanish silver coins, worth about $.20.

luck. It was deep midnight before his anxious mind could settle itself into sleep. Again the golden dream was repeated, and again he saw his garden teeming with ingots and money bags.

Wolfert rose the next morning in complete bewilderment. A dream, three times repeated, was never known to lie, and if so, his fortune was made.

In his agitation he put on his waistcoat with the hind part before, and this was a corroboration of good luck.[13] He no longer doubted that a huge store of money lay buried somewhere in his cabbage field, coyly waiting to be sought for, and he repined at having so long been scratching about the surface of the soil instead of digging to the center.

He took his seat at the breakfast table, full of these speculations, asked his daughter to put a lump of gold into his tea, and on handing his wife a plate of slapjacks, begged her to help herself to a doubloon.

---

[13] It is an old superstition that to put on one's clothes wrong side out forebodes good luck.

His grand care now was how to secure this immense treasure without its being known. Instead of his working regularly in his grounds in the daytime, he now stole from his bed at night, and with spade and pickax went to work to rip up and dig about his paternal acres, from one end to the other. In a little time the whole garden, which had presented such a goodly and regular appearance, with its phalanx of cabbages, like a vegetable army in battle array, was reduced to a scene of devastation, while the relentless Wolfert, with nightcap on head and lantern and spade in hand, stalked through the slaughtered ranks, the destroying angel of his own vegetable world.

Every morning bore testimony to the ravages of the preceding night in cabbages of all ages and conditions, from the tender sprout to the full-grown head, piteously rooted from their quiet beds like worthless weeds, and left to wither in the sunshine. In vain Wolfert's wife remonstrated; in vain his darling daughter wept over the destruction of some favorite marigold. "Thou shalt have gold of another-guess[14] sort," he would cry, chucking her under the chin; "thou shalt have a string of crooked ducats for thy wedding necklace, my child." His family began really to fear that the poor man's wits were diseased. He muttered in his sleep at night about mines of wealth, about pearls and diamonds, and bars of gold. In the daytime he was moody and abstracted, and walked about as if in a trance. Dame Webber held frequent councils with all the old women of the neighborhood; scarce an hour in the day but a knot of them might be seen wagging their white caps together round her door, while the poor woman made some piteous recital. The daughter, too, was fain to seek for more frequent consolation from the stolen interviews of her favored swain, Dirk Waldron. The delectable little Dutch songs with which she used to dulcify the house grew less and less frequent, and she would forget

---

[14] A corruption of the old expression "another-gates," or "of another gate," meaning "of another way or manner"; hence, "of another kind."

her sewing, and look wistfully in her father's face as he sat pondering by the fireside. Wolfert caught her eye one day fixed on him thus anxiously, and for a moment was roused from his golden reveries. "Cheer up, my girl," said he exultingly; "why dost thou droop? Thou shalt hold up thy head one day with the Brinckerhoffs, and the Schermerhorns, the Van Hornes, and the Van Dams.[15] By St. Nicholas, but the patroon[16] himself shall be glad to get thee for his son!"

Amy shook her head at his vainglorious boast, and was more than ever in doubt of the soundness of the good man's intellect.

---

[15] Names of rich and influential Dutch families in the old Dutch colony of New Amsterdam.

[16] The patroons were members of the Dutch West India Company, who purchased land in New Netherlands of the Indians, and after fulfilling certain conditions imposed with a view to colonizing their territory, enjoyed feudal rights similar to those of the barons of the Middle Ages.

In the meantime Wolfert went on digging and digging; but the field was extensive, and as his dream had indicated no precise spot, he had to dig at random. The winter set in before one tenth of the scene of promise had been explored.

The ground became frozen hard, and the nights too cold for the labors of the spade.

No sooner, however, did the returning warmth of spring loosen the soil, and the small frogs begin to pipe in the meadows, but Wolfert resumed his labors with renovated zeal. Still, however, the hours of industry were reversed.

Instead of working cheerily all day, planting and setting out his vegetables, he remained thoughtfully idle, until the shades of night summoned him to his secret labors. In this way he continued to dig from night to night, and week to week, and month to month, but not a stiver[17] did he find. On the contrary, the more he digged the poorer he grew.

---

[17] A Dutch coin, worth about two cents; hence, anything of little worth.

The rich soil of his garden was digged away, and the sand and gravel from beneath was thrown to the surface, until the whole field presented an aspect of sandy barrenness.

In the meantime, the seasons gradually rolled on. The little frogs which had piped in the meadows in early spring croaked as bullfrogs during the summer heats, and then sank into silence. The peach tree budded, blossomed, and bore its fruit. The swallows and martins came, twittered about the roof, built their nests, reared their young, held their congress along the eaves, and then winged their flight in search of another spring. The caterpillar spun its winding sheet, dangled in it from the great buttonwood tree before the house, turned into a moth, fluttered with the last sunshine of summer, and disappeared; and finally the leaves of the buttonwood tree turned yellow, then brown, then rustled one by one to the ground, and whirling about in little eddies of wind and dust, whispered that winter was at hand.

Wolfert gradually woke from his dream of wealth as the year declined.

He had reared no crop for the supply of his household during the sterility of winter. The season was long and severe, and for the first time the family was really straitened in its comforts. By degrees a revulsion of thought took place in Wolfert's mind, common to those whose golden dreams have been disturbed by pinching realities. The idea gradually stole upon him that he should come to want. He already considered himself one of the most unfortunate men in the province, having lost such an incalculable amount of undiscovered treasure, and now, when thousands of pounds had eluded his search, to be perplexed for shillings and pence was cruel in the extreme.

Haggard care gathered about his brow; he went about with a money-seeking air, his eyes bent downward into the dust, and carrying his hands in his pockets, as men are apt to do when they have nothing else to put into them. He could not even pass the city almshouse without giving it a rueful glance, as if destined to be his future abode.

The strangeness of his conduct and of his looks occasioned much speculation and remark. For a long time he was suspected of being crazy, and then everybody pitied him; and at length it began to be suspected that he was poor, and then everybody avoided him.

The rich old burghers of his acquaintance met him outside the door when he called, entertained him hospitably on the threshold, pressed him warmly by the hand at parting, shook their heads as he walked away, with the kindhearted expression of "poor Wolfert," and turned a corner nimbly if by chance they saw him approaching as they walked the streets. Even the barber and the cobbler of the neighborhood, and a tattered tailor in an alley hard by, three of the poorest and merriest rogues in the world, eyed him with that abundant sympathy which usually attends a lack of means, and there is not a doubt but their pockets would have been at his command, only that they happened to be empty.

Thus everybody deserted the Webber mansion, as if poverty were contagious, like the plague – everybody but honest

Dirk Waldron, who still kept up his stolen visits to the daughter, and indeed seemed to wax more affectionate as the fortunes of his mistress were on the wane.

Many months had elapsed since Wolfert had frequented his old resort, the rural inn. He was taking a long, lonely walk one Saturday afternoon, musing over his wants and disappointments, when his feet took instinctively their wonted direction, and on awaking out of a reverie, he found himself before the door of the inn. For some moments he hesitated whether to enter, but his heart yearned for companionship, and where can a ruined man find better companionship than at a tavern, where there is neither sober example nor sober advice to put him out of countenance?

Wolfert found several of the old frequenters of the inn at their usual posts and seated in their usual places; but one was missing, the great Ramm Rapelye, who for many years had filled the leather-bottomed chair of state. His place was supplied by a stranger, who seemed, however, completely at home in the chair and the tavern. He was rather under size, but deep-chested, square, and muscular. His broad shoulders, double joints, and bow knees gave tokens of prodigious strength. His face was dark and weather-beaten; a deep scar, as if from the slash of a cutlass, had almost divided his nose, and made a gash in his upper lip, through which his teeth shone like a bulldog's. A mop of iron-gray hair gave a grisly finish to this hard-favored visage. His dress was of an amphibious character. He wore an old hat edged with tarnished lace, and cocked in martial style on one side of his head; a rusty[18] blue military coat with brass buttons; and a wide pair of short petticoat trousers, – or rather breeches, for they were gathered up at the knees. He ordered everybody about him with an authoritative air, talking in a brattling[19] voice that sounded like the crackling of thorns under a pot, d–d the landlord and servants with perfect

---

[18] Shabby.

[19] Noisy.

impunity, and was waited upon with greater obsequiousness than had ever been shown to the mighty Ramm himself.

Wolfert's curiosity was awakened to know who and what was this stranger who had thus usurped absolute sway in this ancient domain. Peechy Prauw took him aside into a remote corner of the hall, and there, in an under voice and with great caution, imparted to him all that he knew on the subject. The inn had been aroused several months before, on a dark, stormy night, by repeated long shouts that seemed like the howlings of a wolf. They came from the water side, and at length were distinguished to be hailing the house in the seafaring manner, "House ahoy!" The landlord turned out with his head waiter, tapster, hostler, and errand boy – that is to say, with his old negro Cuff. On approaching the place whence the voice proceeded, they found this amphibious-looking personage at the water's edge, quite alone, and seated on a great oaken sea chest. How he came there, – whether he had been set on shore from some boat, or had floated to land on his chest, – nobody could tell, for he did not seem disposed to answer questions, and there was something in his looks and manners that put a stop to all questioning. Suffice it to say, he took possession of a corner room of the inn, to which his chest was removed with great difficulty. Here he had remained ever since, keeping about the inn and its vicinity. Sometimes, it is true, he disappeared for one, two, or three days at a time, going and returning without giving any notice or account of his movements. He always appeared to have plenty of money, though often of very strange, outlandish coinage, and he regularly paid his bill every evening before turning in.

He had fitted up his room to his own fancy, having slung a hammock from the ceiling instead of a bed, and decorated the walls with rusty pistols and cutlasses of foreign workmanship. A greater part of his time was passed in this room, seated by the window, which commanded a wide view of the Sound, a short, old-fashioned pipe in his mouth, a glass of rum toddy[20] at his elbow, and a pocket telescope in his hand, with which he reconnoitered every boat that moved upon the water. Large square-rigged vessels seemed to excite but little attention; but the moment he descried anything with a shoulder-of-mutton[21] sail, or that a barge or yawl or jolly-boat hove in sight, up went the telescope, and he examined it with the most scrupulous attention.

All this might have passed without much notice, for in those times the province was so much the resort of adventurers of all characters and climes that any oddity in dress or behavior attracted but small attention. In a little while, however, this strange sea monster, thus strangely cast upon dry land, began to encroach upon the long established customs and customers of the place, and to interfere in a dictatorial manner in the affairs of the

---

[20] A mixture of rum and hot water sweetened.

[21] Triangular.

ninepin alley and the barroom, until in the end he usurped an absolute command over the whole inn. It was all in vain to attempt to withstand his authority. He was not exactly quarrelsome, but boisterous and peremptory, like one accustomed to tyrannize on a quarterdeck; and there was a dare-devil[22] air about everything he said and did that inspired wariness in all bystanders. Even the half-pay officer, so long the hero of the club, was soon silenced by him, and the quiet burghers stared with wonder at seeing their inflammable man of war so readily and quietly extinguished.

And then the tales that he would tell were enough to make a peaceable man's hair stand on end. There was not a sea fight, nor marauding nor freebooting adventure that had happened within the last twenty years, but he seemed perfectly versed in it. He delighted to talk of the exploits of the buccaneers in the West Indies and

---

22 Reckless.

on the Spanish Main.[23] How his eyes would glisten as he described the waylaying of treasure ships; the desperate fights, yardarm[24] and yardarm, broadside and broadside;[25] the boarding and capturing huge Spanish galleons! With what chuckling relish would he describe the descent upon some rich Spanish colony, the rifling of a church, the sacking of a convent! You would have thought you heard some gormandizer dilating upon the roasting

---

[23] The coast of the northern part of South America along the Caribbean Sea, the route formerly traversed by the Spanish treasure ships between the Old and New Worlds.

[24] Ships are said to be yardarm and yardarm when so near as to touch or interlock their yards, which are the long pieces of timber designed to support and extend the square sails.

[25] "Broadside and broadside," i.e., with the side of one ship touching that of another.

of a savory goose at Michaelmas,[26] as he described the roasting of some Spanish don to make him discover his treasure, – a detail given with a minuteness that made every rich old burgher present turn uncomfortably in his chair. All this would be told with infinite glee, as if he considered it an excellent joke, and then he would give such a tyrannical leer in the face of his next neighbor that the poor man would be fain to laugh out of sheer faintheartedness. If anyone, however, pretended to contradict him in any of his stories, he was on fire in an instant. His very cocked hat assumed a momentary fierceness, and seemed to resent the contradiction. "How the devil should you know as well as I? I tell you it was as I say;" and he would at the same time let slip a broadside of thundering oaths[27] and tremendous sea

---

26 The Feast of the Archangel Michael, a church festival celebrated on September 29th.

27 "Broadside of thundering oaths," i.e., a volley of abuse.

phrases, such as had never been heard before within these peaceful walls.

Indeed, the worthy burghers began to surmise that he knew more of those stories than mere hearsay. Day after day their conjectures concerning him grew more and more wild and fearful. The strangeness of his arrival, the strangeness of his manners, the mystery that surrounded him, – all made him something incomprehensible in their eyes. He was a kind of monster of the deep to them; he was a merman, he was a behemoth, he was a leviathan, – in short, they knew not what he was.

The domineering spirit of this boisterous sea urchin at length grew quite intolerable. He was no respecter of persons; he contradicted the richest burghers without hesitation; he took possession of the sacred elbow chair, which time out of mind had been the seat of sovereignty of the illustrious Ramm Rapelye. Nay, he even went so far, in one of his rough, jocular moods, as to slap that mighty burgher on the back, drink his toddy, and wink in his face, – a thing scarcely to be believed. From this time Ramm Rapelye appeared no more at the inn. His example was followed by several of the most eminent customers, who were too rich to tolerate being bullied out of their opinions or being obliged to laugh at another man's jokes. The landlord was almost in despair; but he knew not how to get rid of this sea monster and his sea chest, who seemed both to have grown like fixtures, or excrescences on his establishment.

Such was the account whispered cautiously in Wolfert's ear by the narrator, Peechy Prauw, as he held him by the button in a corner of the hall, casting a wary glance now and then toward the door of the barroom, lest he should be overheard by the terrible hero of his tale.

Wolfert took his seat in a remote part of the room in silence, impressed with profound awe of this unknown, so versed in freebooting history. It was to him a wonderful instance of the revolutions of mighty empires, to find the venerable Ramm Rapelye thus ousted from the throne, and a rugged tarpaulin[28] dictating from his elbow chair, hectoring the patriarchs, and filling this tranquil little realm with brawl and bravado.

The stranger was, on this evening, in a more than usually communicative mood, and was narrating a number of astounding stories of plunderings and burnings on the high seas. He dwelt upon them with peculiar relish, heightening the frightful particulars in proportion to their effect on his peaceful auditors. He gave a swaggering detail of the capture of a Spanish merchantman. She was lying becalmed during a long summer's day, just off from the island which was one of the lurking places of the pirates. They had reconnoitered her with their spyglasses from the shore, and ascertained her character and force. At night a picked crew of daring fellows set off for her in a whaleboat. They approached with muffled oars, as she lay rocking idly with the undulations of the sea, and her sails flapping against the masts.

---

28 A kind of canvas used about a ship; hence, a sailor.

They were close under the stern before the guard on deck was aware of their approach. The alarm was given; the pirates threw hand grenades[29] on deck, and sprang up the main chains,[30] sword in hand.

The crew flew to arms, but in great confusion; some were shot down, others took refuge in the tops, others were driven overboard and drowned, while others fought hand to hand from the main deck to the quarterdeck, disputing gallantly every inch of ground. There were three Spanish gentlemen on board, with their ladies, who made the most desperate resistance. They defended the

---

29 "Hand grenades," i.e., small shells of iron or glass filled with gunpowder and thrown by hand.

30 "Main chains," i.e., strong bars of iron bolted at the lower end to the side of a vessel, and secured at the upper end to the iron straps of the blocks by which the shrouds supporting the masts are extended.

companion way,[31] cut down several of their assailants, and fought like very devils, for they were maddened by the shrieks of the ladies from the cabin. One of the dons was old, and soon dispatched. The other two kept their ground vigorously, even though the captain of the pirates was among their assailants. Just then there was a shout of victory from the main deck. "The ship is ours!" cried the pirates.

One of the dons immediately dropped his sword and surrendered; the other, who was a hotheaded youngster, and just married, gave the captain a slash in the face that laid all open. The captain just made out to articulate the words, "No quarter."

"And what did they do with their prisoners?" said Peechy Prauw eagerly.

"Threw them all overboard," was the answer. A dead pause followed the reply. Peechy Prauw sank quietly back, like a man who had unwarily stolen upon the lair of a sleeping lion. The honest burghers cast fearful glances at

---

[31] The companion way is a staircase leading to the cabin of a ship.

the deep scar slashed across the visage of the stranger, and moved their chairs a little farther off. The seaman, however, smoked on without moving a muscle, as though he either did not perceive, or did not regard, the unfavorable effect he had produced upon his hearers.

The half-pay officer was the first to break the silence, for he was continually tempted to make ineffectual head against this tyrant of the seas, and to regain his lost consequence in the eyes of his ancient companions. He now tried to match the gunpowder tales of the stranger by others equally tremendous. Kidd, as usual, was his hero, concerning whom he seemed to have picked up many of the floating traditions of the province. The seaman had always evinced a settled pique against the one-eyed warrior. On this occasion he listened with peculiar impatience. He sat with one arm akimbo, the other elbow on the table, the hand holding on to the small pipe he was pettishly puffing, his legs crossed, drumming with one foot on the ground, and casting every now and then the side glance of a basilisk at the prosing captain. At length the latter spoke of Kidd's having ascended the Hudson with some of his crew, to land his plunder in secrecy.

Kidd up the Hudson!" burst forth the seaman, with a tremendous oath; "Kidd never was up the Hudson!"

"I tell you he was," said the other. "Aye, and they say he buried a quantity of treasure on the little flat that runs out into the river, called the Devil's Dans Kammer."[32]

"The Devil's Dans Kammer in your teeth!"[33] cried the seaman. "I tell you Kidd never was up the Hudson. What a plague do you know of Kidd and his haunts?"

"What do I know?" echoed the half-pay officer. "Why, I was in London at the time of his trial; aye, and I had the pleasure of seeing him hanged at Execution Dock."

---

[32] A huge, flat rock, projecting into the Hudson River above the Highlands.

[33] "In your teeth," a phrase to denote direct opposition or defiance.

"Then, sir, let me tell you that you saw as pretty a fellow hanged as ever trod shoe leather. Aye!" putting his face nearer to that of the officer, "and there was many a landlubber[34] looked on that might much better have swung in his stead."

The half-pay officer was silenced; but the indignation thus pent up in his bosom glowed with intense vehemence in his single eye, which kindled like a coal.

Peechy Prauw, who never could remain silent, observed that the gentleman certainly was in the right. Kidd never did bury money up the Hudson, nor indeed in any of those parts, though many affirmed such to be the fact. It was Bradish[35] and others of

---

34 A term of contempt used by seamen for those who pass their lives on land.

35 Bradish was a pirate whose actions were blended in the popular mind with those of Kidd. He was boatswain of a ship which sailed from England in 1697, and which, like Kidd's, bore the name of the Adventure. In the absence of the captain on shore, he seized the ship and set out

the buccaneers who had buried money, some said in Turtle Bay,[36] others on Long Island, others in the neighborhood of Hell Gate. "Indeed," added he, "I recollect an adventure of Sam, the negro fisherman, many years ago, which some think had something to do with the buccaneers. As we are all friends here, and as it will go no further, I'll tell it to you.

"Upon a dark night many years ago, as Black Sam was returning from fishing in Hell Gate—"

Here the story was nipped in the bud by a sudden movement from the unknown, who, laying his iron fist on the table, knuckles downward, with a quiet force that indented the very boards, and looking grimly over his shoulder, with the grin of an angry

---

on a piratical cruise. After amassing a fortune, he sailed for America and deposited a large amount of his wealth with a confederate on Long Island. He was apprehended in Rhode Island, sent to England, and executed.

[36] A small cove in the East River two miles north of Corlear's Hook.

bear, – "Hearkee, neighbor," said he, with significant nodding of the head, "you'd better let the buccaneers and their money alone; they're not for old men and old women to meddle with. They fought hard for their money – they gave body and soul for it; and wherever it lies buried, depend upon it he must have a tug with the devil who gets it!

This sudden explosion was succeeded by a blank silence throughout the room. Peechy Prauw shrunk within himself, and even the one-eyed officer turned pale. Wolfert, who from a dark corner of the room had listened with intense eagerness to all this talk about buried treasure, looked with mingled awe and reverence at this bold buccaneer, for such he really suspected him to be. There was a chinking of gold and a sparkling of jewels in all his stories about the Spanish Main that gave a value to every period, and Wolfert would have given anything for the rummaging of the ponderous sea chest, which his imagination crammed full of golden chalices, crucifixes, and jolly round bags of doubloons.

The dead stillness that had fallen upon the company was at length interrupted by the stranger, who pulled out a prodigious watch of curious and ancient workmanship, and which in Wolfert's eyes had a decidedly Spanish look. On touching a spring, it struck ten o'clock, upon which the sailor called for his reckoning, and having paid it out of a handful of outlandish coin, he drank off the remainder of his beverage, and without taking leave of anyone, rolled out of the room, muttering to himself as he stamped upstairs to his chamber.

It was some time before the company could recover from the silence into which they had been thrown. The very footsteps of the stranger, which were heard now and then as he traversed his chamber, inspired awe.

Still the conversation in which they had been engaged was too interesting not to be resumed. A heavy thunder gust had gathered up unnoticed while they were lost in talk, and the torrents of rain that fell forbade all thoughts of setting off for home until the storm should subside. They drew nearer together, therefore, and entreated the

worthy Peechy Prauw to continue the tale which had been so discourteously interrupted. He readily complied, whispering, however, in a tone scarcely above his breath, and drowned occasionally by the rolling of the thunder; and he would pause every now and then and listen, with evident awe, as he heard the heavy footsteps of the stranger pacing overhead. The following is the purport of his story:

Adventure of the Black Fisherman

Everybody knows Black Sam, the old negro fisherman, or, as he is commonly called, "Mud Sam," who has fished about the Sound for the last half century. It is now many years since Sam, who was then as active a young negro as any in the province, and worked on the farm of Killian Suydam on Long Island, having finished his day's work at an early hour, was fishing, one still summer evening, just about the neighborhood of Hell Gate.

He was in a light skiff, and being well acquainted with the currents and

eddies, had shifted his station, according to the shifting of the tide, from the Hen and Chickens to the Hog's Back, from the Hog's Back to the Pot, and from the Pot to the Frying Pan; but in the eagerness of his sport he did not see that the tide was rapidly ebbing, until the roaring of the whirlpools and eddies warned him of his danger, and he had some difficulty in shooting his skiff from among the rocks and breakers, and getting to the point of Blackwell's Island.[37] Here he cast anchor for some time, waiting the turn of the tide to enable him to return homeward. As the night set in, it grew blustering and gusty. Dark clouds came bundling up in the west, and now and then a growl of thunder or a flash of lightning told that a summer storm was at hand. Sam pulled over, therefore, under the lee of Manhattan Island, and, coasting along, came to a snug nook, just under a steep, beetling rock, where he fastened his skiff to the root of a tree that shot out from a cleft, and spread its broad

---

[37] A long, narrow island in the East River, between New York and Long Island City.

branches like a canopy over the water. The gust came scouring along, the wind threw up the river in white surges, the rain rattled among the leaves, the thunder bellowed worse than that which is now bellowing, the lightning seemed to lick up the surges of the stream; but Sam, snugly sheltered under rock and tree, lay crouching in his skiff, rocking upon the billows until he fell asleep.

When he woke all was quiet. The gust had passed away, and only now and then a faint gleam of lightning in the east showed which way it had gone. The night was dark and moonless, and from the state of the tide Sam concluded it was near midnight. He was on the point of making loose his skiff to return homeward when he saw a light gleaming along the water from a distance, which seemed rapidly approaching. As it drew near he perceived it came from a lantern in the bow of a boat gliding along under shadow of the land. It pulled up in a small cove close to where he was. A man jumped on shore, and searching about with the lantern, exclaimed, "This is the place – here's the iron ring." The boat was then made fast, and the man, returning on board, assisted his comrades in conveying something heavy on shore. As the light gleamed among them, Sam saw that they were five stout, desperate-looking fellows, in red woolen caps, with a leader in a three-cornered hat, and that some of them were armed with dirks, or long knives, and pistols. They talked low to one another, and occasionally in some outlandish tongue which he could not understand.

On landing they made their way among the bushes, taking turns to relieve each other in lugging their burden up the rocky bank. Sam's curiosity was now fully aroused, so leaving his skiff he clambered silently up a ridge that overlooked their path. They had stopped to rest for a moment, and the leader was looking about among the bushes with his lantern. "Have you brought the spades?" said one. "They are here," replied another, who had them on his shoulder. "We must dig deep, where there will be no risk of discovery," said a third.

A cold chill ran through Sam's veins. He fancied he saw before him a gang of murderers, about to bury their victim. His knees smote together. In his agitation he shook the branch of a tree with which he was supporting himself as he looked over the edge of the cliff.

"What's that?" cried one of the gang. "Some one stirs among the bushes!"

The lantern was held up in the direction of the noise. One of the redcaps cocked a pistol, and pointed it toward the very place where Sam was standing. He stood motionless, breathless, expecting the next moment to be his last. Fortunately his dingy complexion was in his favor, and made no glare among the leaves.

"'Tis no one," said the man with the lantern. "What a plague! you would not fire off your pistol and alarm the country!"

The pistol was uncocked, the burden was resumed, and the party slowly toiled along the bank. Sam watched them as they went, the light sending back fitful gleams through the dripping bushes, and it was not till they were fairly out of sight that he ventured to draw breath freely. He now thought of getting back to his boat, and making his escape out of the reach of such dangerous neighbors; but curiosity was all-powerful. He hesitated, and lingered, and listened. By and by he heard the strokes of spades. "They are digging the grave!" said he to himself, and the cold sweat started upon his forehead. Every stroke of a spade, as it sounded through the silent groves, went to his heart. It was evident there was as little noise made as possible; everything had an air of terrible mystery and secrecy. Sam had a great relish for the horrible; a tale of murder was a treat for him, and he was a constant attendant at executions. He could not resist an impulse, in spite of every danger, to steal nearer to the scene of mystery, and overlook the midnight fellows at their work. He crawled along cautiously, therefore, inch by inch, stepping with the utmost care among the dry leaves, lest their rustling should betray him. He came at length to where a steep rock intervened between him and the gang, for he saw the light of their lantern shining up against the branches of the trees on the other side. Sam slowly and silently clambered up the surface of the rock, and raising his head above its naked edge, beheld the villains immediately below him, and so near that though he dreaded discovery he dared not withdraw lest the least movement should be heard. In this way he remained, with his round black face peering above the edge of the rock, like the sun just emerging above the edge of the horizon, or the round-cheeked moon on the dial of a clock.

The redcaps had nearly finished their work, the grave was filled up, and they were carefully replacing the turf. This done they scattered dry leaves over the place. "And now," said the leader, "I defy the devil himself to find it out."

"The murderers!" exclaimed Sam involuntarily.

The whole gang started, and looking up beheld the round black head of Sam just above them, his white eyes strained half out of their orbits, his white teeth chattering, and his whole visage shining with cold perspiration.

"We're discovered!" cried one.

"Down with him!" cried another.

Sam heard the cocking of a pistol, but did not pause for the report. He scrambled over rock and stone, through brush and brier, rolled down banks like a hedgehog, scrambled up others like a catamount. In every direction he heard some one or other of the gang hemming him in. At length he reached the rocky ridge along the river; one of the redcaps was hard behind him. A steep rock like a wall rose directly in his way; it seemed to cut off all retreat, when fortunately he espied the strong, cordlike branch of a grapevine reaching half way down it. He sprang at it with the force of a desperate man, seized it with both hands, and, being young and agile, succeeded in swinging himself to the summit of the cliff. Here he stood in full relief against the sky, when the redcap cocked his pistol and fired. The ball whistled by Sam's head. With the lucky thought of a man in an emergency, he uttered a yell, fell to the ground, and detached at the same time a fragment of the rock, which tumbled with a loud splash into the river.

"I've done his business," said the Redcap to one or two of his comrades as they arrived panting. "He'll tell no tales, except to the fishes in the river."

His pursuers now turned to meet their companions. Sam, sliding silently down the surface of the rock, let himself quietly into his skiff, cast loose the fastening, and abandoned himself to the rapid current, which in that place runs like a mill stream, and soon swept him off from the neighborhood. It was not, however, until he had drifted a great distance that he ventured to ply his oars, when he made his skiff dart like an arrow through the strait of Hell Gate, never heeding the danger of Pot, Frying Pan, nor Hog's Back itself, nor did he feel himself thoroughly secure until safely nestled in bed in the cockloft of the ancient farmhouse of the Suydams.

Here the worthy Peechy Prauw paused to take breath, and to take a sip of the gossip tankard that stood at his elbow. His auditors remained with open mouths and outstretched necks, gaping like a nest of swallows for an additional mouthful.

"And is that all?" exclaimed the half-pay officer.

"That's all that belongs to the story," said Peechy Prauw.

"And did Sam never find out what was buried by the redcaps?" said Wolfert eagerly, whose mind was haunted by nothing but ingots and doubloons.

"Not that I know of," said Peechy; "he had no time to spare from his work, and, to tell the truth, he did not like to run the risk of another race among the rocks. Besides, how should he recollect the spot where the grave had been digged? everything would look so different by daylight. And then, where was the use of looking for a dead body when there was no chance of hanging the murderers?"

"Aye, but are you sure it was a dead body they buried?" said Wolfert.

"To be sure," cried Peechy Prauw exultingly. "Does it not haunt in the neighborhood to this very day?"

"Haunts!" exclaimed several of the party, opening their eyes still wider, and edging their chairs still closer.

"Aye, haunts," repeated Peechy; "have none of you heard of Father Redcap, who haunts the old burned farmhouse in the woods, on the border of the Sound, near Hell Gate?"

"Oh, to be sure, I've heard tell of something of the kind, but then I took it for some old wives' fable."

"Old wives' fable or not," said Peechy Prauw, "that farmhouse stands hard by the very spot. It's been unoccupied time out of mind, and stands in a lonely part of the coast, but those who fish in the neighborhood have often heard strange noises there, and lights have been seen about the wood at night, and an old fellow in a red cap has been seen at the windows more than once, which people take to be the ghost of the body buried there. Once upon a time three soldiers took shelter in the building for the night, and rummaged it from top to bottom, when they found old Father Redcap astride of a cider barrel in the cellar, with a jug in one hand and a goblet in the other. He offered them a drink out of his goblet, but just as one of the soldiers was putting it to his mouth – whew! –

a flash of fire blazed through the cellar, blinded every mother's son of them for several minutes, and when they recovered their eyesight, jug, goblet, and Redcap had vanished, and nothing but the empty cider barrel remained."

Here the half-pay officer, who was growing very muzzy and sleepy, and nodding over his liquor, with half-extinguished eye, suddenly gleamed up like an expiring rush-light.

"That's all fudge!" said he, as Peechy finished his last story.

"Well, I don't vouch for the truth of it myself," said Peechy Prauw, "though all the world knows that there's something strange about that house and grounds; but as to the story of Mud Sam, I believe it just as well as if it had happened to myself."

The deep interest taken in this conversation by the company had made them unconscious of the uproar abroad among the elements, when suddenly they were electrified by a tremendous clap of thunder. A lumbering crash followed instantaneously, shaking the building to its very foundation. All started from their seats, imagining it the shock of an earthquake, or that old Father Redcap was coming among them in all his terrors. They listened for a moment, but only heard the rain pelting against the windows and the wind howling among the trees. The explosion was soon explained by the apparition of an old negro's bald head thrust in at the door, his white goggle eyes contrasting with his jetty poll, which was wet with rain, and shone like a bottle. In a jargon but half intelligible he announced that the kitchen chimney had been struck with lightning.

A sullen pause of the storm, which now rose and sank in gusts, produced a momentary stillness. In this interval the report of a musket was heard, and a long shout, almost like a yell, resounded from the shores. Everyone crowded to the window; another musket shot was heard, and another long shout, mingled wildly with a rising blast of wind. It seemed as if the cry came up from the bosom of the waters, for though incessant flashes of lightning spread a light about the shore, no one was to be seen.

Suddenly the window of the room overhead was opened, and a loud halloo uttered by the mysterious stranger. Several hailings passed from one party to the other, but in a language which none of the company in the barroom could understand, and presently they heard the window closed, and a great noise overhead, as if all the furniture were pulled and hauled about the room. The negro servant was summoned, and shortly afterwards was seen assisting the veteran to lug the ponderous sea chest downstairs.

The landlord was in amazement. "What, you are not going on the water in such a storm?"

"Storm!" said the other scornfully, "do you call such a sputter of weather a storm?"

"You'll get drenched to the skin; you'll catch your death!" said Peechy Prauw affectionately.

"Thunder and lightning!" exclaimed the veteran; "don't preach about weather to a man that has cruised in whirlwinds and tornadoes."

The obsequious Peechy was again struck dumb. The voice from the water was heard once more in a tone of impatience; the bystanders stared with redoubled awe at this man of storms, who seemed to have come up out of the deep, and to be summoned back to it again. As, with the assistance of the negro, he slowly bore his ponderous sea chest toward the shore, they eyed it with a superstitious feeling, half doubting whether he were not really about to embark upon it and launch forth upon the wild waves. They followed him at a distance with a lantern.

"Dowse[38] the light!" roared the hoarse voice from the water. "No one wants light here!"

"Thunder and lightning!" exclaimed the veteran, turning short upon them; "back to the house with you!"

Wolfert and his companions shrank back in dismay. Still their curiosity would not allow them entirely to withdraw. A long sheet of lightning now flickered across the waves, and discovered a boat, filled with men, just

---

[38] Extinguish.

under a rocky point, rising and sinking with the heaving surges, and swashing the waters at every heave. It was with difficulty held to the rocks by a boat hook, for the current rushed furiously round the point. The veteran hoisted one end of the lumbering sea chest on the gunwale of the boat, and seized the handle at the other end to lift it in, when the motion propelled the boat from the shore, the chest slipped off from the gunwale, and, sinking into the waves, pulled the veteran headlong after it. A loud shriek was uttered by all on shore, and a volley of execrations by those on board, but boat and man were hurried away by the rushing swiftness of the tide. A pitchy darkness succeeded. Wolfert Webber, indeed, fancied that he distinguished a cry for help, and that he beheld the drowning man beckoning for assistance; but when the lightning again gleamed along the water all was void; neither man nor boat was to be seen, – nothing but the dashing and weltering of the waves as they hurried past.

The company returned to the tavern to await the subsiding of the storm.

They resumed their seats and gazed on each other with dismay. The whole transaction had not occupied five minutes, and not a dozen words had been spoken. When they looked at the oaken chair they could scarcely realize the fact that the strange being who had so lately tenanted it, full of life and Herculean vigor, should already be a corpse. There was the very glass he had just drunk from; there lay the ashes from the pipe which he had smoked, as it were, with his last breath. As the worthy burghers pondered on these things, they felt a terrible conviction of the uncertainty of existence, and each felt as if the ground on which he stood was rendered less stable by his awful example.

As, however, the most of the company were possessed of that valuable philosophy which enables a man to bear up with fortitude against the misfortunes of his neighbors, they soon managed to console themselves for the tragic end of the veteran. The landlord was particularly happy that the poor dear man had paid his reckoning before he went, and made a kind of farewell speech on the occasion.

"He came," said he, "in a storm, and he went in a storm; he came in the night, and he went in the night; he came nobody knows whence, and he has gone nobody knows where. For aught I know he has gone to sea once more on his chest, and may land to bother some people on the other side of the world; though it's a thousand pities," added he, "if he has gone to Davy Jones's[39] locker, that he had not left his own locker[40] behind him."

"His locker! St. Nicholas preserve us!" cried Peechy Prauw. "I'd not have had that sea chest in the house for any money; I'll warrant he'd come racketing after it at nights, and making a haunted house of the inn. And as to his going to sea in his chest, I recollect what

---

[39] Davy Jones is the spirit of the sea, or the sea devil, and Davy Jones's locker is the bottom of the ocean; hence, "gone to Davy Jones's locker" signifies "dead and buried in the sea."

[40] Chest.

happened to Skipper Onderdonk's ship on his voyage from Amsterdam.

"The boatswain died during a storm, so they wrapped him up in a sheet, and put him in his own sea chest, and threw him overboard; but they neglected, in their hurry-skurry, to say prayers over him, and the storm raged and roared louder than ever, and they saw the dead man seated in his chest, with his shroud for a sail, coming hard after the ship, and the sea breaking before him in great sprays like fire; and there they kept scudding day after day and night after night, expecting every moment to go to wreck; and every night they saw the dead boatswain in his sea chest trying to get up with them, and they heard his whistle above the blasts of wind, and he seemed to send great seas, mountain high, after them that would have swamped the ship if they had not put up the deadlights. And so it went on till they lost sight of him in the fogs off Newfoundland, and supposed he had veered ship and stood for Dead Man's Isle.[41] So much for burying a man at sea without saying prayers over him."

The thunder gust which had hitherto detained the company was now at an end. The cuckoo clock in the hall told midnight; everyone pressed to depart, for seldom was such a late hour of the night trespassed on by these quiet burghers. As they sallied forth they found the heavens once more serene. The storm which had lately obscured them had rolled away, and lay piled up in fleecy masses on the horizon, lighted up by the bright crescent of the moon, which looked like a little silver lamp hung up in a palace of clouds.

The dismal occurrence of the night, and the dismal narrations they had made, had left a superstitious feeling in every mind. They cast a fearful glance at the spot where the buccaneer had disappeared, almost expecting to see him sailing on his chest in the cool moonshine. The trembling rays glittered

---

[41] Probably Deadman's Point, a small island near Deadman's Bay, off the eastern coast of Newfoundland.

along the waters, but all was placid, and the current dimpled over the spot where he had gone down. The party huddled together in a little crowd as they repaired homeward, particularly when they passed a lonely field where a man had been murdered, and even the sexton, who had to complete his journey alone, though accustomed, one would think, to ghosts and goblins, went a long way round rather than pass by his own churchyard.

Wolfert Webber had now carried home a fresh stock of stories and notions to ruminate upon. These accounts of pots of money and Spanish treasures, buried here and there and everywhere about the rocks and bays of these wild shores, made him almost dizzy. "Blessed St. Nicholas!" ejaculated he, half aloud, "is it not possible to come upon one of these golden hoards, and to make oneself rich in a twinkling? How hard that I must go on, delving and delving, day in and day out, merely to make a morsel of bread, when one lucky stroke of a spade might enable me to ride in my carriage for the rest of my life!"

As he turned over in his thoughts all that had been told of the singular adventure of the negro fisherman, his imagination gave a totally different complexion[42] to the tale. He saw in the gang of redcaps nothing but a crew of pirates burying their spoils, and his cupidity was once more awakened by the possibility of at length getting on the traces of some of this lurking wealth. Indeed, his infected fancy tinged everything with gold. He felt like the greedy inhabitant of Bagdad when his eyes had been greased with the magic ointment of the dervish, that gave him to see all the treasures of the earth.[43]

---

[42] Aspect.

[43] See Story of the Blind Man, Baba Abdalla, in Arabian Nights' Entertainment. An inhabitant of Bagdad, Asiatic Turkey, meets with a dervish, or Turkish monk, who presents him with a vast treasure and with a box of magic ointment, which, applied to the left eye, enables one to see the treasures in the bosom of the earth, but on touching the right eye, causes blindness. Having applied it to the left eye with the result predicted, he uses it on his right eye, in the hope that still

Caskets of buried jewels, chests of ingots, and barrels of outlandish coins seemed to court him from their concealments, and supplicate him to relieve them from their untimely graves.

On making private inquiries about the grounds said to be haunted by Feather Redcap, he was more and more confirmed in his surmise. He learned that the place had several times been visited by experienced money diggers who had heard Black Sam's story, though none of them had met with success. On the contrary, they had always been dogged with ill luck of some kind or other, in consequence, as Wolfert concluded, of not going to work at the proper time and with the proper ceremonials. The last attempt had been made by Cobus Quackenbos, who dug for a whole night, and met with incredible difficulty, for as fast as he threw one shovelful of earth out of the hole, two were thrown in by invisible hands. He succeeded so far, however, as to uncover an iron chest, when there

greater treasures may be revealed, and immediately becomes blind.

was a terrible roaring, ramping, and raging of uncouth figures about the hole, and at length a shower of blows, dealt by invisible cudgels, fairly belabored him off of the forbidden ground. This Cobus Quackenbos had declared on his deathbed, so that there could not be any doubt of it. He was a man that had devoted many years of his life to money digging, and it was thought would have ultimately succeeded had he not died recently of a brain fever in the almshouse.

Wolfert Webber was now in a worry of trepidation and impatience, fearful lest some rival adventurer should get a scent of the buried gold. He determined privately to seek out the black fisherman, and get him to serve as guide to the place where he had witnessed the mysterious scene of interment. Sam was easily found, for he was one of those old habitual beings that live about a neighborhood until they wear themselves a place in the public mind, and become, in a manner, public characters. There was not an unlucky urchin about town that did not know Sam the fisherman, and think that

he had a right to play his tricks upon the old negro. Sam had led an amphibious life for more than half a century, about the shores of the bay and the fishing grounds of the Sound. He passed the greater part of his time on and in the water, particularly about Hell Gate, and might have been taken, in bad weather, for one of the hobgoblins that used to haunt that strait. There would he be seen, at all times and in all weathers, sometimes in his skiff, anchored among the eddies, or prowling like a shark about some wreck, where the fish are supposed to be most abundant; sometimes seated on a rock from hour to hour, looking, in the mist and drizzle, like a solitary heron watching for its prey. He was well acquainted with every hole and corner of the Sound, from the Wallabout[44] to Hell Gate, and from Hell Gate unto the Devil's stepping-stones; and it was even affirmed that he knew all the fish in the river by their Christian names.

---

[44] A bay of the East River, on which the Brooklyn Navy Yard is situated.

Wolfert found him at his cabin, which was not much larger than a tolerable dog house. It was rudely constructed of fragments of wrecks and driftwood, and built on the rocky shore at the foot of the old fort, just about what at present forms the point of the Battery.[45] A "very ancient and fishlike smell"[46] pervaded the place. Oars, paddles, and fishing rods were leaning against the wall of the fort, a net was spread on the sand to dry, a skiff was drawn up on the beach, and at the door of his cabin was Mud Sam himself, indulging in the true negro luxury of sleeping in the sunshine.

Many years had passed away since the time of Sam's youthful adventure, and the snows of many a winter had grizzled the knotty wool upon his head. He perfectly recollected the circumstances, however, for he had often been called upon to relate them, though in his version of the story he

---

[45] The southern extremity of New York City.

[46] See Shakespeare's The Tempest, act ii., sc. 2.

differed in many points from Peechy Prauw, as is not infrequently the case with authentic historians. As to the subsequent researches of money diggers, Sam knew nothing about them; they were matters quite out of his line; neither did the cautious Wolfert care to disturb his thoughts on that point. His only wish was to secure the old fisherman as a pilot to the spot, and this was readily effected. The long time that had intervened since his nocturnal adventure had effaced all Sam's awe of the place, and the promise of a trifling reward roused him at once from his sleep and his sunshine.

The tide was adverse to making the expedition by water, and Wolfert was too impatient to get to the land of promise to wait for its turning; they set off, therefore, by land. A walk of four or five miles brought them to the edge of a wood, which at that time covered the greater part of the eastern side of the island. It was just beyond the pleasant region of Bloomen-dael.[47] Here

---

47 At the time this story was written Bloomen-dael (Flowery Valley) was a

they struck into a long lane, straggling among trees and bushes very much overgrown with weeds and mullein stalks, as if but seldom used, and so completely overshadowed as to enjoy but a kind of twilight. Wild vines entangled the trees and flaunted in their faces; brambles and briers caught their clothes as they passed; the garter snake glided across their path; the spotted toad hopped and waddled before them; and the restless catbird mewed at them from every thicket. Had Wolfert Webber been deeply read in romantic legend he might have fancied himself entering upon forbidden, enchanted ground, or that these were some of the guardians set to keep watch upon buried treasure. As it was, the loneliness of the place, and the wild stories connected with it, had their effect upon his mind.

On reaching the lower end of the lane they found themselves near the

village four miles from New York. It is now that part of New York known as Bloomingdale, on the west side, between about Seventieth and One Hundredth Streets.

shore of the Sound, in a kind of amphitheater surrounded by forest trees. The area had once been a grass plot, but was now shagged with briers and rank weeds. At one end, and just on the river bank, was a ruined building, little better than a heap of rubbish, with a stack of chimneys rising like a solitary tower out of the center. The current of the Sound rushed along just below it, with wildly grown trees drooping their branches into its waves.

Wolfert had not a doubt that this was the haunted house of Father Redcap, and called to mind the story of Peechy Prauw. The evening was approaching, and the light, falling dubiously among the woody places, gave a melancholy tone to the scene well calculated to foster any lurking feeling of awe or superstition. The night hawk, wheeling about in the highest regions of the air, emitted his peevish, boding cry. The woodpecker gave a lonely tap now and then on some hollow tree, and the firebird[48] streamed by them with his deep red plumage.

They now came to an inclosure that had once been a garden. It extended along the foot of a rocky ridge, but was little better than a wilderness of weeds, with here and there a matted rosebush, or a peach or plum tree, grown wild and ragged, and covered with moss. At the lower end of the garden they passed a kind of vault in the side of a bank, facing the water. It had the look of a root house.[49] The door, though decayed, was still strong, and appeared to have been recently patched up. Wolfert pushed it open. It gave a harsh grating upon its hinges, and striking against something like a box, a rattling sound ensued, and a skull rolled on the floor. Wolfert drew back shuddering, but was reassured on being informed by the negro that this was a family vault, belonging to one of the old Dutch

---

48 Orchard oriole.

49 "Root house," i.e., a house for storing up potatoes, turnips, or other roots for the winter feed of cattle.

families that owned this estate, an assertion corroborated by the sight of coffins of various sizes piled within. Sam had been familiar with all these scenes when a boy, and now knew that he could not be far from the place of which they were in quest.

They now made their way to the water's edge, scrambling along ledges of rocks that overhung the waves, and obliged often to hold by shrubs and grapevines to avoid slipping into the deep and hurried stream. At length they came to a small cove, or rather indent of the shore. It was protected by steep rocks, and overshadowed by a thick copse of oaks and chestnuts, so as to be sheltered and almost concealed. The beach shelved gradually within the cove, but, the current swept deep and black and rapid along its jutting points. The negro paused, raised his remnant of a hat, and scratched his grizzled poll for a moment, as he regarded this nook; then suddenly clapping his hands, he stepped exultingly forward, and pointed to a large iron ring, stapled firmly in the rock, just where a broad shelf of stone furnished a commodious landing place. It was the very spot where the redcaps had landed. Years had changed the more perishable features of the scene; but rock and iron yield slowly to the influence of time. On looking more closely Wolfert remarked three crosses cut in the rock just above the ring, which had no doubt some mysterious signification. Old Sam now readily recognized the overhanging rock under which his skiff had been sheltered during the thunder gust. To follow up the course which the midnight gang had taken, however, was a harder task. His mind had been so much taken up on that eventful occasion by the persons of the drama as to pay but little attention to the scenes, and these places looked so different by night and day. After wandering about for some time, however, they came to an opening among the trees which Sam thought resembled the place. There was a ledge of rock of moderate height, like a wall, on one side, which he thought might be the very ridge whence he had overlooked the diggers. Wolfert examined it narrowly, and at length discovered three crosses similar to those on the above ring, cut deeply into the face of the rock, but nearly obliterated by moss that had grown over them. His heart leaped with joy, for he doubted not they were the private marks of the buccaneers. All now that remained was to ascertain the precise spot where the treasure lay buried, for otherwise he might dig at random in the neighborhood of the crosses, without coming upon the spoils, and he had already had enough of such profitless labor. Here, however, the old negro was perfectly at a loss, and indeed perplexed him by a variety of opinions, for his recollections were all confused. Sometimes he declared it must have been at the foot of a mulberry tree hard by; then beside a great white stone; then under a small green knoll, a short distance from the ledge of rocks, until at length Wolfert became as bewildered as himself.

The shadows of evening were now spreading themselves over the woods, and rock and tree began to mingle together. It was evidently too late to attempt anything further at present, and, indeed, Wolfert had come unprovided with implements to prosecute his researches. Satisfied, therefore, with having ascertained the place, he took note of all its landmarks, that he might recognize it again, and set out on his return homeward, resolved to prosecute this golden enterprise without delay.

The leading anxiety which had hitherto absorbed every feeling being now in some measure appeased, fancy began to wander, and to conjure up a thousand shapes and chimeras as he returned through this haunted region. Pirates hanging in chains seemed to swing from every tree, and he almost expected to see some Spanish don, with his throat cut from ear to ear, rising slowly out of the ground, and shaking the ghost of a money bag.

Their way back lay through the desolate garden, and Wolfert's nerves had arrived at so sensitive a state that the flitting of a bird, the rustling of a leaf, or the falling of a nut was enough to startle him. As they entered the confines of the garden, they caught sight of a figure at a distance advancing slowly up one of the walks, and bending under the weight of a burden. They paused and regarded him attentively. He wore what appeared to be a woolen cap, and, still more alarming, of a most sanguinary red.

The figure moved slowly on, ascended the bank, and stopped at the very door of the sepulchral vault. Just before entering it he looked around. What was the affright of Wolfert when he recognized the grisly visage of the drowned buccaneer! He uttered an ejaculation of horror. The figure slowly raised his iron fist and shook it with a terrible menace. Wolfert did not pause to see any more, but hurried off as fast as his legs could carry him, nor was Sam slow in following at his heels, having all his ancient terrors revived. Away, then, did they scramble through bush and brake, horribly frightened at every bramble that tugged at their skirts, nor did they pause to breathe until they had blundered their way through this perilous wood, and fairly reached the highroad to the city.

Several days elapsed before Wolfert could summon courage enough to prosecute the enterprise, so much had he been dismayed by the apparition, whether living or dead, of the grisly buccaneer. In the meantime, what a conflict of mind did he suffer! He neglected all his concerns, was moody and restless all day, lost his appetite, wandered in his thoughts and words, and committed a thousand blunders. His rest was broken, and when he fell asleep the nightmare, in shape of a huge money bag, sat squatted upon his breast. He babbled about incalculable sums, fancied himself engaged in money digging, threw the bedclothes right and left, in the idea that he was shoveling away the dirt, groped under the bed in quest of the treasure, and lugged forth, as he supposed, an inestimable pot of gold.

Dame Webber and her daughter were in despair at what they conceived a returning touch of insanity. There are two family oracles, one or other of which Dutch housewives consult in all cases of great doubt and perplexity, – the dominie and the doctor. In the present instance they repaired to the doctor. There was at that time a little dark, moldy man of medicine, famous among the old wives of the Manhattoes for his skill, not only in the healing art, but in all matters of strange and mysterious nature. His name was Dr. Knipperhausen, but he was more commonly known by the appellation of the "High German Doctor."[50] To him did the poor women repair for counsel and assistance touching the mental vagaries of Wolfert Webber.

They found the doctor seated in his little study, clad in his dark camlet[51] robe of knowledge, with his black velvet cap, after the manner of Boerhaave,[52] Van Helmont,[53] and other medical sages, a pair of green spectacles set in black horn upon his clubbed nose, and poring

---

50 The same, no doubt, of whom mention is made in the history of Dolph Heyliger.

51 A fabric made of goat's hair and silk, or wool and cotton.

52 Hermann Boerhaave (1668-1738), a celebrated Dutch physician and philosopher.

53 Jan Baptista Van Helmont (1577-1644), a celebrated Flemish physician and chemist.

over a German folio that reflected back the darkness of his physiognomy. The doctor listened to their statement of the symptoms of Wolfert's malady with profound attention, but when they came to mention his raving about buried money the little man pricked up his ears. Alas, poor women! they little knew the aid they had called in.

Dr. Knipperhausen had been half his life engaged in seeking the short cuts to fortune, in quest of which so many a long lifetime is wasted. He had passed some years of his youth among the Harz[54] mountains of Germany, and had derived much valuable instruction from the miners touching the mode of seeking treasure buried in the earth. He had prosecuted his studies, also, under a traveling sage who united the mysteries of medicine with magic and legerdemain. His mind, therefore, had become stored with all kinds of mystic lore; he had dabbled a little in

---

[54] A mountain chain in northwestern Germany, between the Elbe and the Weser.

astrology, alchemy, divination;[55] knew how to detect stolen money, and to tell where springs of water lay hidden; in a word, by the dark nature of his knowledge he had acquired the name of the "High German Doctor," which is pretty nearly equivalent to that of necromancer. The doctor had often heard rumors of treasure being buried in various parts of the island, and had long been anxious to get on the traces of it. No sooner were Wolfert's waking and sleeping vagaries confided to him than he beheld in them the confirmed symptoms of a case of money digging, and lost no time in probing it to the bottom. Wolfert had long been sorely oppressed in mind by the golden secret, and as a family physician is a kind of

---

55 Astrology, alchemy, and divination were three imaginary arts. The first pretended to judge of the influence of the stars on human affairs, and to foretell events by their positions and aspects; the second aimed to transmute the baser metals into gold, and to find a universal remedy for diseases; while the third dealt with the discovery of secret or future events by preternatural means.

father confessor, he was glad of any opportunity of unburdening himself. So far from curing, the doctor caught the malady from his patient. The circumstances unfolded to him awakened all his cupidity; he had not a doubt of money being buried somewhere in the neighborhood of the mysterious crosses, and offered to join Wolfert in the search. He informed him that much secrecy and caution must be observed in enterprises of the kind; that money is only to be dug for at night, with certain forms and ceremonies and burning of drugs, the repeating of mystic words, and, above all, that the seekers must first be provided with a divining rod,[56] which had the wonderful property of pointing to the very spot on the surface of the earth under which treasure lay hidden. As the doctor had given much of his mind to these matters he charged himself with all the necessary preparations, and, as the

---

56 A divining rod is a rod used by those who pretend to discover water or metals underground. It is commonly made of witch hazel, with forked branches.

quarter of the moon was propitious, he undertook to have the divining rod ready by a certain night.

Wolfert's heart leaped with joy at having met with so learned and able a coadjutor. Everything went on secretly but swimmingly. The doctor had many consultations with his patient, and the good women of the household lauded the comforting effect of his visits. In the meantime the wonderful divining rod, that great key to nature's secrets, was duly prepared. The doctor had thumbed over all his books of knowledge for the occasion, and the black fisherman was engaged to take them in his skiff to the scene of enterprise, to work with spade and pickax in unearthing the treasure, and to freight his bark with the weighty spoils they were certain of finding.

At length the appointed night arrived for this perilous undertaking. Before Wolfert left his home he counseled his wife and daughter to go to bed, and feel no alarm if he should not return during the night. Like reasonable women, on being told not to feel alarm they fell immediately into a panic. They saw at once by his manner that something unusual was in agitation; all their fears about the unsettled state of his mind were revived with tenfold force; they hung about him, entreating him not to expose himself to the night air, but all in vain. When once Wolfert was mounted on his hobby,[57] it was no easy manner to get him out of the saddle. It was a clear, starlight night when he issued out of the portal of the Webber palace. He wore a large flapped hat, tied under the chin with a handkerchief of his daughter's, to secure him from the night damp, while Dame Webber threw her long red cloak about his shoulders, and fastened it round his neck.

The doctor had been no less carefully armed and accoutered by his housekeeper, the vigilant Frau Ilsy, and sallied forth in his camlet robe by way of surcoat,[58] his black velvet cap under

---

[57] Hobby, or hobbyhorse, a favorite theme of thought; hence, "to mount a hobby" is to follow a favorite pursuit.

[58] Overcoat.

his cocked hat, a thick clasped book under his arm, a basket of drugs and dried herbs in one hand, and in the other the miraculous rod of divination.

The great church clock struck ten as Wolfert and the doctor passed by the churchyard, and the watchman bawled in hoarse voice a long and doleful "All's well!" A deep sleep had already fallen upon this primitive little burgh; nothing disturbed this awful silence excepting now and then the bark of some profligate, night-walking dog, or the serenade of some romantic cat. It is true Wolfert fancied more than once that he heard the sound of a stealthy footfall at a distance behind them; but it might have been merely the echo of their own steps along the quiet streets. He thought also at one time that he saw a tall figure skulking after them, stopping when they stopped and moving on as they proceeded; but the dim and uncertain lamplight threw such vague gleams and shadows that this might all have been mere fancy.

They found the old fisherman waiting for them, smoking his pipe in the stern of the skiff, which was moored just in front of his little cabin. A pickax and spade were lying in the bottom of the boat, with a dark lantern, and a stone bottle of good Dutch courage,[59] in which honest Sam no doubt put even more faith than Dr. Knipperhausen in his drugs.

Thus, then, did these three worthies embark in their cockleshell of a skiff upon this nocturnal expedition, with a wisdom and valor equaled only by the three wise men of Gotham,*[60] who adventured to sea in a bowl. The tide was rising and running rapidly up the Sound. The current bore them along, almost without the aid of an oar. The profile of the town lay all in shadow. Here and there a light feebly glimmered from some sick chamber, or from the cabin window of some vessel at anchor

---

[59] Dutch courage is courage that results from indulgence in Dutch gin or Hollands; here applied to the gin itself.

[60] Gotham was a village proverbial for the blundering simplicity of its inhabitants. At first the name referred to an English village. Irving applied it to New York City.

in the stream. Not a cloud obscured the deep, starry firmament, the lights of which wavered on the surface of the placid river, and a shooting meteor, streaking its pale course in the very direction they were taking, was interpreted by the doctor into a most propitious omen.

[* "Three wise men of Gotham,
They went to sea in a bowl–
And if the bowl had been stronger,
My tale had been longer."
"– Mother Goose Melody"]

In a little while they glided by the point of Corlear's Hook, with the rural inn which had been the scene of such night adventures. The family had retired to rest, and the house was dark and still. Wolfert felt a chill pass over him as they passed the point where the buccaneer had disappeared. He pointed it out to Dr. Knipperhausen. While regarding it they thought they saw a boat actually lurking at the very place; but the shore cast such a shadow over the border of the water that they could discern nothing distinctly. They had not proceeded far when they heard the low sounds of distant oars, as if cautiously pulled. Sam plied his oars with redoubled vigor, and knowing all the eddies and currents of the stream, soon left their followers, if such they were, far astern. In a little while they stretched across Turtle Bay and Kip's Bay,[61] then shrouded themselves in the deep shadows of the Manhattan shore, and glided swiftly along, secure from observation. At length the negro shot his skiff into a little cove, darkly embowered by trees, and made it fast to the well-known iron ring. They now landed, and lighting the lantern gathered their various implements and proceeded slowly through the bushes. Every sound startled them, even that of their own footsteps among the dry leaves, and the hooting of a screech owl, from the shattered chimney of the neighboring ruin, made their blood run cold.

In spite of all Wolfert's caution in taking note of the landmarks, it was some time before they could find the

---

61 A small bay in the East River below Corlear's Hook.

open place among the trees, where the treasure was supposed to be buried. At length they came to the ledge of rock, and on examining its surface by the aid of the lantern, Wolfert recognized the three mystic crosses. Their hearts beat quick, for the momentous trial was at hand that was to determine their hopes.

The lantern was now held by Wolfert Webber, while the doctor produced the divining rod. It was a forked twig, one end of which was grasped firmly in each hand, while the center, forming the stem, pointed perpendicularly upward. The doctor moved his wand about, within a certain distance of the earth, from place to place, but for some time without any effect, while Wolfert kept the light of the lantern turned full upon it, and watched it with the most breathless interest. At length the rod began slowly to turn. The doctor grasped it with greater earnestness, his hands trembling with the agitation of his mind. The wand continued to turn gradually, until at length the stem had reversed its position, and pointed perpendicularly downward, and remained pointing to one spot as fixedly as the needle to the pole.

"This is the spot!" said the doctor, in an almost inaudible tone.

Wolfert's heart was in his throat.

"Shall I dig?" said the negro, grasping the spade.

"Pots tausend,[62] no!" replied the little doctor hastily. He now ordered his companions to keep close by him, and to maintain the most inflexible silence; that certain precautions must be taken and ceremonies used to prevent the evil spirits which kept about buried treasure from doing them any harm. He then drew a circle about the place, enough to include the whole party. He next gathered dry twigs and leaves and made a fire, upon which he threw certain drugs and dried herbs which he had brought in his basket. A thick smoke rose, diffusing a potent odor savoring marvelously of brimstone and asafetida, which, however grateful it might be to the olfactory nerves of spirits, nearly strangled poor Wolfert,

---

62 A German exclamation of anger, equivalent to the English "zounds!"

and produced a fit of coughing and wheezing that made the whole grove resound. Dr. Knipperhausen then unclasped the volume which he had brought under his arm, which was printed in red and black characters in German text. While Wolfert held the lantern, the doctor, by the aid of his spectacles, read off several forms of conjuration in Latin and German. He then ordered Sam to seize the pickax and proceed to work. The close-bound soil gave obstinate signs of not having been disturbed for many a year. After having picked his way through the surface, Sam came to a bed of sand and gravel, which he threw briskly to right and left with the spade.

"Hark!" said Wolfert, who fancied he heard a trampling among the dry leaves and a rustling through the bushes. Sam paused for a moment, and they listened. No footstep was near. The bat flitted by them in silence; a bird, roused from its roost by the light which glared up among the trees, flew circling about the flame. In the profound stillness of the woodland they could distinguish the current rippling along the rocky shore, and the distant murmuring and roaring of Hell Gate.

The negro continued his labors, and had already digged a considerable hole. The doctor stood on the edge, reading formulae every now and then from his black-letter volume, or throwing more drugs and herbs upon the fire, while Wolfert bent anxiously over the pit, watching every stroke of the spade. Anyone witnessing the scene thus lighted up by fire, lantern, and the reflection of Wolfert's red mantle, might have mistaken the little doctor for some foul magician, busied in his incantations, and the grizzly-headed negro for some swart goblin obedient to his commands.

At length the spade of the fisherman struck upon something that sounded hollow. The sound vibrated to Wolfert's heart. He struck his spade again.

"'Tis a chest," said Sam.

"Full of gold, I'll warrant it!" cried Wolfert, clasping his hands with rapture.

Scarcely had he uttered the words when a sound from above caught his ear. He cast up his eyes, and lo! by the expiring light of the fire he beheld, just over the disk of the rock, what appeared to be the grim visage of the drowned buccaneer, grinning hideously down upon him.

Wolfert gave a loud cry and let fall the lantern. His panic communicated itself to his companions. The negro leaped out of the hole, the doctor dropped his book and basket, and began to pray in German. All was horror and confusion. The fire was scattered about, the lantern extinguished. In their hurry-scurry[63] they ran against and confounded one another. They fancied a legion of hobgoblins let loose upon them, and that they saw, by the fitful gleams of the scattered embers, strange figures, in red caps, gibbering and ramping around them. The doctor ran one way, the negro another, and Wolfert made for the water side. As he plunged struggling onward through brush and brake, he heard the tread of some one in pursuit. He scrambled frantically forward. The footsteps gained upon him. He felt himself grasped by his cloak, when suddenly his pursuer

---

63 A swift, disorderly movement.

was attacked in turn; a fierce fight and struggle ensued, a pistol was discharged that lit up rock and bush for a second, and showed two figures grappling together; all was then darker than ever. The contest continued, the combatants clinched each other, and panted and groaned, and rolled among the rocks. There was snarling and growling as of a cur, mingled with curses, in which Wolfert fancied he could recognize the voice of the buccaneer. He would fain have fled, but he was on the brink of a precipice, and could go no farther.

Again the parties were on their feet, again there was a tugging and struggling, as if strength alone could decide the combat, until one was precipitated from the brow of the cliff, and sent headlong into the deep stream that whirled below. Wolfert heard the plunge, and a kind of strangling, bubbling murmur, but the darkness of the night hid everything from him, and the swiftness of the current swept everything instantly out of hearing. One of the combatants was disposed of, but whether friend or foe Wolfert could not tell, nor whether they might not both be foes. He heard the survivor approach, and his terror revived. He saw, where the profile of the rocks rose against the horizon, a human form advancing. He could not be mistaken; it must be the buccaneer. Whither should he fly? – a precipice was on one side, a murderer on the other. The enemy approached – he was close at hand. Wolfert attempted to let himself down the face of the cliff. His cloak caught in a thorn that grew on the edge. He was jerked from off his feet, and held dangling in the air, half choked by the string with which his careful wife had fastened the garment around his neck. Wolfert thought his last moment was arrived; already had he committed his soul to St. Nicholas, when the string broke, and he tumbled down the bank, bumping from rock to rock and bush to bush, and leaving the red cloak fluttering like a bloody banner in the air.

It was a long while before Wolfert came to himself. When he opened his eyes, the ruddy streaks of morning were already shooting up the sky. He found himself grievously battered, and lying in the bottom of a boat. He attempted to sit up, but was too sore and stiff to move. A voice requested him in a friendly accents to lie still. He turned his eyes toward the speaker; it was Dirk Waldron. He had dogged the party, at the earnest request of Dame Webber and her daughter, who, with the laudable curiosity of their sex, had pried into the secret consultations of Wolfert and the doctor. Dirk had been completely distanced in following the light skiff of the fisherman, and had just come in time to rescue the poor money digger from his pursuer.

Thus ended this perilous enterprise. The doctor and Black Sam severally found their way back to the Manhattoes, each having some dreadful tale of peril to relate. As to poor Wolfert, instead of returning in triumph, laden with bags of gold, he was borne home on a shutter, followed by a rabble-rout[64] of curious urchins. His wife and daughter saw the dismal pageant from a distance, and alarmed the neighborhood with their

---

64 A noisy throng.

cries; they thought the poor man had suddenly settled the great debt of nature in one of his wayward moods. Finding him, however, still living, they had him speedily to bed, and a jury of old matrons of the neighborhood assembled to determine how he should be doctored. The whole town was in a buzz with the story of the money diggers. Many repaired to the scene of the previous night's adventures; but though they found the very place of the digging, they discovered nothing that compensated them for their trouble. Some say they found the fragments of an oaken chest, and an iron pot lid, which savored strongly of hidden money, and that in the old family vault there were traces of bales and boxes; but this is all very dubious.

In fact, the secret of all this story has never to this day been discovered. Whether any treasure were ever actually buried at that place; whether, if so, it were carried off at night by those who had buried it; or whether it still remains there under the guardianship of gnomes and spirits until it shall be properly sought for, is all matter of conjecture.

For my part, I incline to the latter opinion, and make no doubt that great sums lie buried, both there and in other parts of this island and its neighborhood, ever since the times of the buccaneers and the Dutch colonists; and I would earnestly recommend the search after them to such of my fellow citizens as are not engaged in any other speculations.

There were many conjectures formed, also, as to who and what was the strange man of the seas, who had domineered over the little fraternity at Corlear's Hook for a time, disappeared so strangely, and reappeared so fearfully. Some supposed him a smuggler stationed at that place to assist his comrades in landing their goods among the rocky coves of the island. Others, that he was one of the ancient comrades of Kidd or Bradish, returned to convey away treasures formerly hidden in the vicinity. The only circumstance that throws anything like a vague light on this mysterious matter is a report which prevailed of a strange, foreign-built shallop, with much the look of a picaroon,[65] having been seen hovering about the Sound for several days without landing or reporting herself, though boats were seen going to and from her at night; and that she was seen standing out of the mouth of the harbor, in the gray of the dawn, after the catastrophe of the money diggers.

I must not omit to mention another report, also, which I confess is rather apocryphal, of the buccaneer who is supposed to have been drowned, being seen before daybreak, with a lantern in his hand, seated astride of his great sea chest, and sailing through Hell Gate, which just then began to roar and bellow with redoubled fury.

While all the gossip world was thus filled with talk and rumor, poor Wolfert lay sick and sorrowfully in his bed, bruised in body and sorely beaten down in mind. His wife and daughter did all they could to bind up his wounds, both corporal and spiritual. The good old dame never stirred from his bedside,

---

65 A piratical vessel.

where she sat knitting from morning till night, while his daughter busied herself about him with the fondest care. Nor did they lack assistance from abroad. Whatever may be said of the desertion of friends in distress, they had no complaint of the kind to make. Not an old wife of the neighborhood but abandoned her work to crowd to the mansion of Wolfert Webber, to inquire after his health and the particulars of his story. Not one came, moreover, without her little pipkin of pennyroyal, sage, balm, or other herb tea, delighted at an opportunity of signalizing her kindness and her doctorship. What drenchings did not the poor Wolfert undergo, and all in vain! It was a moving sight to behold him wasting away day by day, growing thinner and thinner and ghastlier and ghastlier, and staring with rueful visage from under an old patchwork counterpane, upon the jury of matrons kindly assembled to sigh and groan and look unhappy around him.

Dirk Waldron was the only being that seemed to shed a ray of sunshine into this house of mourning. He came in with cheery look and manly spirit, and tried to reanimate the expiring heart of the poor money digger, but it was all in vain. Wolfert was completely done over.[66] If anything was wanting to complete his despair, it was a notice, served upon him in the midst of his distress, that the corporation was about to run a new street through the very center of his cabbage garden. He now saw nothing before him but poverty and ruin; his last reliance, the garden of his forefathers, was to be laid waste, and what then was to become of his poor wife and child?

His eyes filled with tears as they followed the dutiful Amy out of the room one morning. Dirk Waldron was seated beside him; Wolfert grasped his hand, pointed after his daughter, and for the first time since his illness broke the silence he had maintained.

"I am going!" said he, shaking his head feebly, "and when I am gone, my poor daughter–"

---

66 Exhausted.

"Leave her to me, father!" said Dirk manfully; "I'll take care of her!"

Wolfert looked up in the face of the cheery, strapping youngster, and saw there was none better able to take care of a woman.

"Enough," said he, "she is yours! And now fetch me a lawyer – let me make my will and die."

The lawyer was brought, – a dapper, bustling, round-headed little man, Roorback (or Rollebuck, as it was pronounced) by name. At the sight of him the women broke into loud lamentations, for they looked upon the signing of a will as the signing of a death warrant. Wolfert made a feeble motion for them to be silent. Poor Amy buried her face and her grief in the bed curtain. Dame Webber resumed her knitting to hide her distress, which betrayed itself, however, in a pellucid tear, which trickled silently down, and hung at the end of her peaked nose; while the cat, the only unconcerned member of the family, played with the good dame's ball of worsted as it rolled about the floor.

Wolfert lay on his back, his nightcap drawn over his forehead, his eyes closed, his whole visage the picture of death. He begged the lawyer to be brief, for he felt his end approaching, and that he had no time to lose. The lawyer nibbed[67] his pen, spread out his paper, and prepared to write.

"I give and bequeath," said Wolfert faintly, "my small farm—"

"What! all?" exclaimed the lawyer.

Wolfert half opened his eyes and looked upon the lawyer.

"Yes, all," said he.

"What! all that great patch of land with cabbages and sunflowers, which the corporation is just going to run a main street through?"

"The same," said Wolfert, with a heavy sigh, and sinking back upon his pillow.

"I wish him joy that inherits it!" said the little lawyer, chuckling and rubbing his hands involuntarily.

"What do you mean?" said Wolfert, again opening his eyes.

---

67 In Irving's time, quills were made into pens by pointing or "nibbing" their ends.

"That he'll be one of the richest men in the place," cried little Rollebuck.

The expiring Wolfert seemed to step back from the threshold of existence; his eyes again lighted up; he raised himself in his bed, shoved back his red worsted nightcap, and stared broadly at the lawyer.

"You don't say so!" exclaimed he.

"Faith but I do!" rejoined the other. "Why, when that great field and that huge meadow come to be laid out in streets and cut up into snug building lots, – why, whoever owns it need not pull off his hat to the patroon!"

"Say you so?" cried Wolfert, half thrusting one leg out of bed; "why, then, I think I'll not make my will yet."

To the surprise of everybody the dying man actually recovered. The vital spark, which had glimmered faintly in the socket, received fresh fuel from the oil of gladness which the little lawyer poured into his soul. It once more burned up into a flame.

Give physic to the heart, ye who would revive the body of a spirit-broken man! In a few days Wolfert left his room; in a few days more his table was covered with deeds, plans of streets and building lots. Little Rollebuck was constantly with him, his right hand man and adviser, and instead of making his will assisted in the more agreeable task of making his fortune. In fact Wolfert Webber was one of those worthy Dutch burghers of the Manhattoes whose fortunes have been made, in a manner, in spite of themselves; who have tenaciously held on to their hereditary acres, raising turnips and cabbages about the skirts of the city, hardly able to make both ends meet, until the corporation has cruelly driven streets through their abodes, and they have suddenly awakened out of their lethargy, and, to their astonishment, found themselves rich men.

Before many months had elapsed a great, bustling street passed through the very center of the Webber garden, just where Wolfert had dreamed of finding a treasure. His golden dream was accomplished; he did, indeed, find an unlooked-for source of wealth, for, when his paternal lands were distributed into building lots and rented out to safe tenants, instead of producing a paltry crop of cabbages they returned him an abundant crop of rent, insomuch that on quarter day it was a goodly sight to see his tenants knocking at the door from morning till night, each with a little round-bellied bag of money, a golden produce of the soil.

The ancient mansion of his forefathers was still kept up, but, instead of being a little yellow-fronted Dutch house in a garden, it now stood boldly in the midst of a street, the grand home of the neighborhood; for Wolfert enlarged it with a wing on each side, and a cupola or tea room on top, where he might climb up and smoke his pipe in hot weather, and in the course of time the whole mansion was overrun by the chubby-faced progeny of Amy Webber and Dirk Waldron.

As Wolfert waxed old and rich and corpulent he also set up a great gingerbread-colored carriage, drawn by a pair of black Flanders mares with tails that swept the ground; and to commemorate the origin of his greatness he had for his crest a full-blown cabbage painted on the panels, with the pithy motto, ALLES

KOPF, that is to say, ALL HEAD, meaning thereby that he had risen by sheer head work.

To fill the measure of his greatness, in the fullness of time the renowned Ramm Rapelye slept with his fathers, and Wolfert Webber succeeded to the leather-bottomed armchair in the inn parlor at Corlear's Hook; where he long reigned, greatly honored and respected, insomuch that he was never known to tell a story without its being believed, nor to utter a joke without its being laughed at.